Menopause and the Workplace

By Daniel Barnett

The Employment Law Library

All books in the Employment Law Library are sent for free to members of the HR Inner Circle.

1. Employee Investigations
2. GDPR for HR Professionals
3. Preventing and Defending Employee Stress Claims
4. Employment Tribunal Time Limits
5. Deconstructing TUPE
6. Changing Terms & Conditions
7. Constructive Dismissal
8. Resolving Grievances
9. HR Hazards
10. Employment Status
11. Spotting Malingering
12. Employment Tribunal Compensation
13. Hiring Staff
14. Computer and Social Media Misuse
15. Managing Sickness Absence
16. The Three Ps
17. Conflict at Work
18. SOSR Dismissals
19. Dismissing Problem Employees
20. Menopause and the Workplace
21. Dismissing Senior Executives
22. Negotiating Exit Packages and Settlement Agreements

Published by Employment Law Services Limited, Unit 3, Chequers Farm, Chequers Lane, Watford, Hertfordshire WD25 0LG

ISBN 978-1-913925-18-5

EMPLOYMENT LAW MATTERS

Subscribe to
Daniel Barnett's podcast

EMPLOYMENT LAW MATTERS

via iTunes, Spotify, or your
favourite podcast player

WWW.DANIELBARNETT.CO.UK/PODCAST

iTunes Spotify

Acknowledgments

Welcome to book 20 in this series of mini guides on employment law for HR professionals.

My main thanks go to Fran Read for her help with the first draft of this book.

Thanks also to Tincuta Collett for the layout and design, Aaron Gaff for proofreading, Marla Ocampo for her edits and Maria Rodriguez for converting the book into the formats needed for Amazon.

None of these books are possible without the input and experience of the members of the HR Inner Circle. I write these small books for you, and you get them for free as part of your membership.

If you're not a member of the HR Inner Circle and you're interested in learning more about membership (www.hrinnercircle.co.uk), there is some information at the back of this book.

Daniel Barnett
January 2025

About the Author

Daniel Barnett is a leading employment law barrister practising from Outer Temple Chambers. With 25 years' experience defending public and private sector employers against employment claims, he has represented a Royal Family, several international airlines, FTSE-100 companies and various NHS Trusts and local authorities. Employee clients include David & Victoria Beckham's nanny and Paul Mason (subject of the ITV documentary 'Britain's Fattest Man').

Daniel is a past chair of the Employment Lawyers' Association's publishing committee and electronic services working party. He is the author or co-author of eight books, including the Law Society Handbook on Employment Law (currently in its 8th edition). He is the creator of the Employment Law (UK) mailing list, an email alerter bulletin service sending details of breaking news in employment law three times a week to 33,000 recipients.

Legal directories describe him as 'extremely knowledgeable and [he] can absorb pages of instructions at lightning speed', 'involved in a number of highly contentious matters', 'singled out for his work for large blue-chip companies', 'combination of in-depth legal knowledge, pragmatism, quick response times and approachability', 'inexhaustible', 'tenacious', 'knowledgeable', and 'an excellent advocate'.

He is one of the leading speakers and trainers on the employment law and HR circuit. He has presented seminars for the House of Commons, the BBC, Oxford University, HSBC, Barclays Bank, Ocado, and dozens of other organisations in-house. In 2013, 2014, 2016, and 2019 he designed — and was the sole speaker at — the Employment Law MasterClass national tour.

As well as full-time practice as a barrister and speaker, Daniel is the founder of the HR Inner Circle – a membership club for smart, ambitious HR Professionals. In 2007, he co-founded CPD Webinars Ltd, then the UK's leading webinar training company for lawyers, and sold it to Thomson Reuters in 2011. Daniel is widely sought after as a commentator in both broadcast and print media on all legal issues. Since 2010 he has presented the Legal Hour on LBC Radio. In 2019, he launched Employment Law Matters, a weekly podcast with short explanations of employment law topics. Subscribe at www.danielbarnett.co.uk/podcast

www.danielbarnett.co.uk
Temple, London

Contents

Chapter 1
Introduction

Claire, a senior manager at a leading tech firm, had always been on top of her game. But in her early 50s, she started noticing changes – sleepless nights, brain fog and unexpected mood swings that disrupted her performance. Despite years of experience, she found herself struggling to keep up. She began to wonder if it was her age catching up with her. It wasn't until a colleague mentioned the word 'menopause' that Claire realised what was happening.

Claire's experience is far from unique. In 2023, the Chartered Institute of Personnel and Development (CIPD) reported that there were almost four million women aged 45 to 55 in employment in the UK, many of them navigating the challenges of menopause. Women over 50 are the fastest-growing workforce demographic in the UK.[1]

This all adds up to the fact that, for HR professionals, understanding and supporting employees through this stage is no longer a luxury – it's a necessity.

This book provides HR professionals with the knowledge and tools needed to navigate the complexities of menopause in the workplace effectively.

The significance of understanding and supporting menopause in the workplace cannot be overstated. Menopause,

---

1 Information taken from the *House of Commons Women and Equalities Committee Report on Menopause and the Workplace*, 19 July 2022.

a natural stage in every woman's life, typically occurs between the ages of 45 and 55. It is characterised by a range of symptoms, including hot flushes, sleep disturbances and mood swings, which can affect an individual's performance, engagement and overall wellbeing at work.

The legal rules around menopause at work are evolving. If employers don't provide proper support, they could face discrimination claims. This makes it essential for HR teams to stay on top of the latest legal standards and take action to protect both employees and the business.

The business case for addressing menopause proactively is compelling. Beyond compliance with legal obligations, there are substantial benefits to be gained from a well-considered approach to menopause in the workplace. These include enhanced employee engagement, reduced absenteeism, improved retention of experienced staff and the promotion of a positive organisational culture. By taking the lead in creating a supportive environment for menopausal employees, businesses can improve their overall performance and competitiveness. The financial implications of ignoring menopause are significant, with the potential for lost productivity, increased turnover and legal costs.

This book explores these themes in detail, providing HR professionals with a comprehensive understanding of the significance of menopause in the workplace, the legal landscape in the UK and the business case for proactive engagement. Through case studies and practical guidance, HR professionals will be equipped to develop and implement strategies for supporting menopausal employees.

For clarity and ease, this book uses the term 'women' when describing the impacts of menopause. Trans men and non-binary people may experience menopause, and references to 'women' should be taken to include all people who may experience menopause. The challenges faced by trans men and non-binary people associated with menopause are explored in more detail in Chapter 2 and Chapter 8.

Chapter 2

Menopause 101 for employers

Of all respondents to the *Women and Equalities Commission's Menopause and the Workforce Survey*, 99% confirmed that they had experienced at least one menopause symptom.[2] What are these symptoms, and how do they affect employees' productivity, well-being and mental health?

This chapter breaks down the science behind menopause, explains its key stages and introduces HR professionals to the real-world challenges that employees face during this transition.

What is menopause?

Menopause is a natural biological process that marks the end of a woman's menstrual cycles and reproductive years, typically occurring between the ages of 45 and 55. It is a significant life stage experienced by half the population, with profound physical, emotional and psychological effects that can impact an individual's daily life, including their work.

According to the NHS,[3] menopause occurs when periods have stopped for over 12 months due to lower hormone levels.

---

2 https://committees.parliament.uk/publications/8995/documents/152634/default/.

3 https://www.nhs.uk/conditions/menopause/

Most of those who experience menopause do so between the ages of 45 and 55. However, some start experiencing symptoms much earlier. Further, some may experience menopause after surgery (such as following a hysterectomy) or after treatment for cancer.

Menopause is preceded by perimenopause, during which periods continue but the body prepares itself for menopause. Perimenopause may involve similar symptoms to menopause and may last months or years. The stage after menopause is known as post-menopause.

In the UK, the average age at which a woman reaches menopause is 51. Sometimes, periods stop suddenly, though usually, they start to become less frequent over a few months or years before they stop altogether. Around one in 100 women experience menopause before the age of 40.[4] This is known as premature menopause or premature ovarian insufficiency. This can be due to surgery, illness or genetic factors.

Does menopause only affect women?

Menopause is fundamentally linked to the function of the ovaries, which produce hormones like oestrogen and progesterone. When the ovaries cease to function or produce these hormones at the levels they did before menopause, menopausal symptoms can occur. This hormonal transition typically happens with age but can also be induced medically or surgically, such as through oophorectomy (the surgical

---

4 Information taken from the *House of Commons Women and Equalities Committee Report on Menopause and the Workplace*, 19 July 2022

removal of the ovaries) or hormone therapy that suppresses oestrogen production.

Some trans men and non-binary people may also experience menopausal symptoms.

For trans men and non-binary individuals who were assigned female at birth and have their ovaries, menopause can bring about the typical symptoms associated with this transition, such as hot flushes, mood changes and sleep disturbances. This experience can be complicated by the fact that these symptoms – and the transition itself – may not align with their gender identity, potentially exacerbating discomfort around their bodies and gender dysphoria (distress caused by a discrepancy between a person's gender identity and their sex assigned at birth).

Common symptoms

Menopause can bring about a range of symptoms that can adversely affect an employee's work life by impacting their productivity, engagement and attendance.

The NHS website[5] explains that most women will experience menopausal symptoms. Some can be severe and have a significant impact on everyday activities. Menopausal symptoms can begin months or even years before a woman's periods stop (perimenopause) and last around four years after her last period, although some women experience them for much longer. Each woman's experience is personal, and symptoms vary in duration, severity and impact.

5 https://www.nhs.uk/conditions/menopause/symptoms/

Symptoms include:

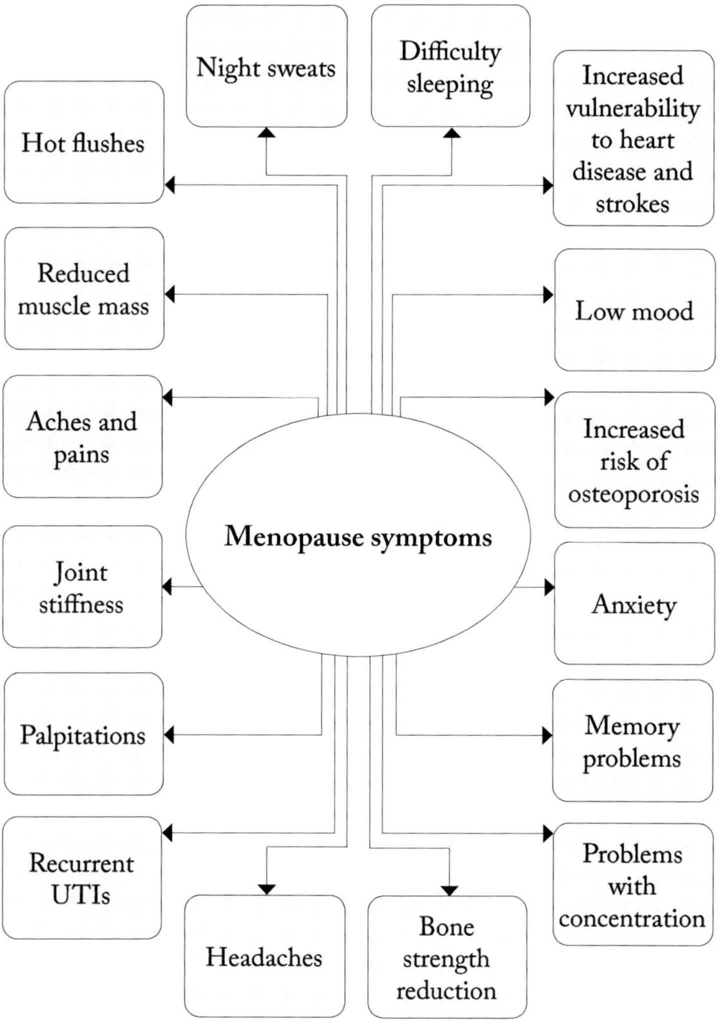

The impact of menopause on mental health

The hormonal changes during menopause can impact mental health. Oestrogen plays a role in regulating mood, and as its levels drop during menopause, women may experience:

- **Anxiety:** Sudden feelings of worry or unease, sometimes without clear triggers.
- **Depression:** A prolonged period of low mood or feelings of worthlessness, which can affect an employee's engagement and productivity.
- **Mood Swings:** Rapid and unpredictable changes in mood, leading to emotional responses that might seem disproportionate to the situation.
- **Cognitive Impairment:** Often referred to as 'brain fog', this includes difficulty concentrating, forgetfulness, and slower mental processing.

Why menopause matters at work

Menopause matters at work because the symptoms can affect an employee's performance and wellbeing. Given the age at which menopause typically occurs, many women are likely to be at a crucial stage in their careers, possibly in senior or demanding roles. Understanding and support from employers during this transition can make a significant difference in their professional and personal lives.

Recognising menopause as a workplace issue is paramount. It is not merely a personal or health issue but a matter of workplace diversity and inclusion. By acknowledging menopause as a significant workplace issue, businesses can take proactive steps to support affected employees, such as implementing flexible working arrangements, providing access to information and resources, and fostering an open and supportive culture.

Chapter 3

The business case for supporting menopausal employees

Imagine losing one of your most experienced team members at the height of their career. Now imagine that nearly 900,000 women have already left the UK workforce because of menopause-related symptoms.[6] The cost? In some cases, it could be over £30,500 per employee to replace them, according to a 2022 study by Oxford Economics.[7]

This chapter explores the fact that supporting menopausal employees isn't just a matter of wellbeing; it's a strategic business imperative.

There are three reasons why it makes sense: it boosts a business's reputation, keeps staff happy and productive, and helps to avoid costly legal trouble.

Reputation

Wellbeing has been a buzzword for businesses for several years now. Businesses recognise the reputational benefits of actively promoting employee wellbeing initiatives. There

6 https://committees.parliament.uk/writtenevidence/39244/html/
7 https://committees.parliament.uk/oralevidence/9793/html/

is a strong reputational benefit for businesses that create menopause-friendly workplaces. Look at the rising profile of the 'Menopause Friendly Employer' accreditation and the 'Menopause Friendly Employer Awards' that are now held annually.

Research by LinkedIn in 2023 found that almost three in five employees wouldn't work for a business that didn't align with their values.[8] An open and supportive position on menopause in the workplace paints a positive picture of a business as an inclusive place.

Productivity, retention and business success

Healthy employees who feel supported are far more productive for businesses than those who are unhealthy and unsupported. This alone should be sufficient to persuade businesses of the importance of supporting menopausal employees.

Absence from work due to menopause symptoms is a key issue. It has a clear and direct impact on productivity and, ultimately, business success. A survey of 1,000 women by Health and Her estimated that menopause costs the UK economy 14 million working days per year, in terms of time spent alleviating menopause symptoms.[9] If employers can support employees through this stage in their lives, absence levels will come down and both the business and the employee will benefit. At the root of this is a need for the business to

8 https://www.personneltoday.com/hr/reject-job-company-values-linkedin-research/

9 https://committees.parliament.uk/writtenevidence/39340/html/

understand menopause and support employees experiencing it.

There is also a significant talent retention problem associated with menopause. The Equality and Human Rights Commission (EHRC) guidance on Menopause in the Workplace[10] reports that one in 10 women who have worked during menopause have left their jobs due to symptoms. Research conducted by the CIPD identified that 60% of women reported that menopausal symptoms have adversely affected their working lives.[11]

A supportive workplace can help to deal with this. Women leaving the workforce because of menopause is alarming for any business.

Oxford Economics suggested in 2022 that if a woman earning £25,000 a year leaves her job due to problematic menopause symptoms, it will cost her employer over £30,500 to replace her.[12]

Beyond the associated cost of recruitment and retraining, losing a female employee because of menopausal symptoms is detrimental to a business's talent pool. Women of this age hold years of experience, knowledge and wisdom. They may be mentoring junior staff, leading teams and setting agendas for the future of the business.

If your business is 'menopause friendly', then you tap into a large talent pool of individuals who are at their professional peak. As of 2023, there are around four million women

10 https://www.equalityhumanrights.com/guidance/menopause-workplace-guidance-employers

11 https://committees.parliament.uk/writtenevidence/39244/html/

12 https://committees.parliament.uk/oralevidence/9793/html/

aged 50 to 64 in employment, and this number is growing. If employers are able to provide clear support to employees experiencing menopause, then they will be best placed to retain this talent for the rest of their working lives. Women are working longer – the average retirement age for women has increased from 60 to 64 in the last 30 years.[13] They have a valuable post-menopausal contribution to make to the workforce as long as employers are able to support them to stay in employment through menopause.

EHRC chairwoman Baroness Kishwer Falkner said:

"As Britain's equality watchdog, we are concerned both by how many women report being forced out of a role due to their menopause-related symptoms and how many don't feel safe enough to request workplace adjustments. An employer understanding their legal duties is the foundation of equality in the workplace."

Legal obligations

This book considers the legal obligations of employers in relation to menopause in Chapters 4 to 10. No business wants to become embroiled in tribunal claims. There is a clear business case for employers to make efforts to support menopausal employees. This reduces the likelihood of claims. Analysis of court records by Menopause Experts Group found that 23 tribunal cases cited menopause in 2021, which was a 44% increase from the 16 cases that cited menopause in 2020. Of these 23 cases, 16 included claims for disability

---

13 https://www.gov.uk/government/statistics/economic-labour-market-status-of-individuals-aged-50-and-over-trends-over-time-september-2021/economic-labour-market-status-of-individuals-aged-50-and-over-trends-over-time-september-2021

discrimination, 14 included claims for unfair dismissal and 10 included claims for sex discrimination. In addition, mentions of the word 'menopause' increased by 75% in tribunal documents.[14]

14 https://menopauseexperts.com/tribunals-triple-in-less-than-2-years/

Chapter 4

Is menopause a disability?

Does menopause count as a disability? For Sarah Donnachie,[15] a simple question turned into a landmark legal case. Her employer claimed her menopause symptoms – sleepless nights, brain fog and physical discomfort – were 'typical' and not serious enough to be a disability. The tribunal thought otherwise, ruling that her symptoms had a 'substantial adverse effect' on her day-to-day life.

This chapter delves into the legal definitions and case law surrounding menopause as a disability, helping HR professionals understand their legal obligations.

It is not 'one size fits all'

It is not the case that every person experiencing menopause symptoms will be a disabled person in the eyes of the law.

Menopause is a natural event that can have varying effects on those experiencing it. Some women will experience very few symptoms at all. Others will suffer substantially. To work out whether an employee's menopause symptoms are a disability, employers need to see if they meet the definition of disability.

15 ET 1300005/2020

EHRC guidance on menopause says:

"If menopause symptoms have a long-term and substantial impact on a woman's ability to carry out normal day-to-day activities, these symptoms could be considered a disability."

Employers need to look at it on a case-by-case basis. Menopause will amount to a disability only if it meets the definition of disability. It should not be assumed that it does.

The definition of disability

Section 6 of the *Equality Act 2010* (EqA 2010) defines a disabled person as a person with a disability. A person has a disability for the purposes of the EqA 2010 if they have a physical or mental impairment and the impairment has a substantial and long-term adverse effect on their ability to carry out normal day-to-day activities.

Gov.uk guidance[16] states that this means that, in general:

- The person must have an impairment that is either physical or mental.
- The impairment must have substantial adverse effects.
- The substantial adverse effects must be long-term.
- The long-term substantial adverse effects must be effects on normal day-to-day activities.

It's important to break this down and apply it to menopause.

16 https://www.gov.uk/definition-of-disability-under-equality-act-2010

1. Physical or mental impairment

Menopause brings with it both physical and mental symptoms. GOV.UK guidance on the definition of disability acknowledges that '*It may not always be possible, nor is it necessary, to categorise a condition as either a physical or a mental impairment.*' There may be adverse effects that are both physical and mental in nature.

When asking whether menopause is a disability, it's important to consider whether menopause-caused impairments meet the definition. It is misleading to focus on menopause itself – this is merely the underlying cause of the impairment. It is the impairment or impairments that must be focused on.

An illustrative example is given in GOV.UK guidance:

"A woman is obese. Her obesity in itself is not an impairment, but it causes breathing and mobility difficulties which substantially adversely affect her ability to walk."

It is the effects of these impairments that need to be considered rather than the underlying condition itself.

2. Substantial adverse effect

The requirement that an adverse effect on normal day-to-day activities should be a substantial one reflects the general understanding of disability as a limitation going beyond the normal differences in ability that may exist among people. A substantial effect is one that is more than a minor or trivial effect. It will be necessary to explore things like the way in which a person carries out a task or the time it takes them to do things.

In *Donnachie v Telent Technology Services Ltd*,[17] the respondent questioned whether menopause symptoms suffered by the claimant were substantial. The claimant gave evidence that her sleep was interrupted, that she avoided walking in warm weather, that she became distracted during conversations and that her pace of reading and writing had reduced. The respondent argued that these were 'typical' menopause symptoms that did not stop her from doing day-to-day activities. The tribunal held that the claimant's symptoms **were** substantial. In doing so, they placed weight on the fact that 'the range of [the claimant's] daily activities and her ability to undertake them when she would wish with the rhythm and frequency she once did is markedly affected'.

It is important to look at the cumulative impact of the effects when deciding whether or not they are substantial. So, for example, a person suffering from breathing difficulties may experience an impact on walking upstairs, travelling on public transport and walking for long distances. The impact of each of these individually may not be substantial but employers should look at them cumulatively when deciding whether the effects are substantial.

3. Long-term effect

An impairment with a long-term effect is one that fits one of the following descriptions:

- Has lasted at least 12 months
- Is likely to last at least 12 months from onset
- Is likely to last for the rest of the person's life

17 ET 1300005/2020

'Likely' means it could well happen. The cumulative effect of related impairments should be considered when determining whether the impairment is long-term. For example, if menopause causes low mood for seven months and then develops into anxiety for six months, these periods are added together to meet the long-term criteria.

It is not necessary for the effect to be the same throughout the period considered. A person may still satisfy the long-term element of the definition even if activities that are initially very difficult become possible. The effect might even disappear temporarily.

4. The ability to carry out normal day-to-day activities

There is no legal definition of 'day-to-day activities'. In general, day-to-day activities are things people do on a daily or regular basis. Examples include shopping, reading and writing, having a conversation or using the telephone, watching television, getting washed and dressed, preparing and eating food, carrying out household tasks, walking and travelling by various forms of transport, and taking part in social activities. Normal day-to-day activities can include general work-related activities as well.

How can an employer know what the symptoms are and what their effect is?

It is sometimes very easy for an employer to see the impact that a condition might have on an employee's life – for example, if an employee is deaf or if they have a physical mobility issue.

The symptoms associated with menopause are a lot harder to tie down as they are often not visible.

Employers should ask the employee to explain the impact of their symptoms, both inside and outside of work. Employees will have the best understanding of their own condition. If employers need more support, they can involve occupational health or get a report from the employee's own doctor or specialist.

This is crucial when deciding necessary adjustments or considering actions influenced by menopause symptoms, such as performance management.

What if the symptoms come and go?

Symptoms of menopause may not be consistent and can come and go. This will not impact whether they meet the definition of disability.

If an impairment has had a substantial adverse effect on a person's ability to carry out normal day-to-day activities but that effect ceases, the substantial effect is treated as continuing if it is likely to recur. Conditions with effects that recur only sporadically or for short periods can still qualify as long-term impairments.

What if the employee is having treatment to manage menopause symptoms?

Employees may be taking medication or having other forms of treatment to manage their menopause symptoms.

If an employee is receiving treatment, the impairment is to be treated as having a substantial adverse effect if, but for the treatment, the impairment is likely to have that effect. The practical effect is that the impairment should be looked at without treatment when considering whether it is a disability. In *Donnachie v Telent Technology Services Ltd*, the tribunal accepted that the claimant used hormone replacement therapy (HRT) patches to treat her menopause symptoms. They said this use should be disregarded when deciding whether her menopause symptoms were a disability.

Measures may go further than traditional medication. They can include receiving counselling and following a particular diet. Correction to eyesight through the use of glasses or contact lenses is, however, specifically excluded.

Should employers treat all women 'of a certain age' as disabled?

Employers need to be clear that each woman's experience of menopause will be different. They should definitely not treat all women 'of a certain age' as disabled. Such a generalised approach is likely to amount to sex and age discrimination. If, for example, an employer adopted a strategy that assumed that all female employees of a certain age had mood swings or suffered from brain fog, then this itself would likely be less favourable treatment on grounds of age and sex.

Employers need to be careful not to make any assumptions about how women will react to menopause.

Guidance from tribunal cases on menopause as a disability

In *Davies v Scottish Courts and Tribunal Service*,[18] the respondent accepted that the claimant was a disabled person by reason of menopause symptoms. In this case, the claimant had suffered from severe bleeding for two to three years, alongside a lack of concentration.

In *Chan v Stansted Airport Ltd*,[19] the respondent contested whether the claimant was disabled as a result of the symptoms of menopause. Employment Judge Park held that the claimant was disabled, explaining:

"The menopause is not in itself an impairment. It is a normal stage in a woman's life. However, women can experience a wide range of symptoms when going through the peri-menopause and menopause. The severity of those symptoms varies, and in some cases, the impact may be such that the woman meets the definition of being disabled under the Equality Act 2010."

The Judge concluded:

"Based on my findings of fact, the menopause symptoms did have a substantial adverse effect on the claimant's ability to carry out normal day-to-day activities at times between July 2017 and when she was dismissed. Some of the symptoms were a lack of concentration, memory loss and fatigue. As a result of these, the claimant forgot information that she usually was able to recall easily. She also found it difficult to concentrate on reading, which included being unable to read a book. As described by the claimant,

18 ET 4104575/2015
19 ET 3205543/2022

these effects are more than minor or trivial. The claimant needed to set up systems to help her remember everyday information that she usually recalled without difficulty. She was unable to read a whole book for several years, having previously done so regularly."

As the Employment Judge made clear, however, all cases need to be assessed individually. There is no assumption that a woman experiencing menopause will be regarded as disabled.

Summary

Whether or not menopause amounts to a disability must be looked at on a case-by-case basis. There is no definitive answer. Employers should think carefully before taking any form of action involving an employee who may be experiencing menopause symptoms. They should consider getting input from occupational health or the employee's own doctor. This will help them understand, from a clinical view, the impact of the employee's condition on their life.

A simple question…

Dear Reader,

Forgive the interruption in flow.

I have a simple question for you...

Would you help an HR Professional you've never met? And, likely, never will?

If 'yes', please keep reading.

If you're reading this book, it's very likely that you're a member of the HR Inner Circle. (If you're not, the HR Inner Circle is a vibrant, active community of HR professionals who want to give like-minded HR Professionals a safe place to get all the help, support, advice and encouragement they need to ease the constant pressure of their job.)

I set up the HR Inner Circle a decade ago, and we have hundreds and hundreds of members.

This is where you come in.

The only way for us at the HR Inner Circle to accomplish our mission is by reaching other HR Professionals, particularly those like you (or like you were a few years ago: less experienced, full of desire to learn, ambitious to succeed, but uncertain were to look).

If you have found this book valuable thus far, would you please take a brief moment right now and leave an honest review of this book and its contents? It will cost you zero pounds and less than 60 seconds.

Your review will help….

- one more HR Professional support a business or an employee;
- one more HR Professional finds find their work meaningful;
- one more HR Professional experience a transformation they otherwise would never have encountered by joining the HR Inner Circle at www.hrinnercircle.co.uk.

To make that happen…

all you have to do is….

(and this takes less than 60 seconds….)

leave a review of this book.

If you are reading a hard copy, you can go to the book page on Amazon and leave a review right on the page. If you are already a member of the HR Inner Circle, you'll have had this book (along with other books in the Employment Law Library) for free as part of your membership – we publish three or four books each year. But you can still leave a review on Amazon (please do!), on goodreads, or even on social media!

Many thanks,
Daniel Barnett

Leave a review >>

Chapter 5
Disability discrimination

Ms Lynskey had worked as a telesales consultant for Direct Line for over five years. As she approached menopause, she started experiencing symptoms, including low mood, anxiety, mood swings, poor self-esteem, effects on memory and poor concentration. These symptoms affected her ability to perform tasks at the same speed and efficiency as before. When her performance began to slip, her employer started a performance management process. Ms Lynskey argued that her employer had not considered the impact of her menopause symptoms on her work performance and had failed to make reasonable adjustments. She took her case to tribunal and won[20], with the tribunal acknowledging that her symptoms amounted to a disability.

The ruling highlights a critical issue: how should employers treat employees whose menopause symptoms significantly impact their work performance?

This chapter explores the different forms of disability discrimination and how menopause fits into this legal framework.

---

20 ET 1802204/2022 and 1802386/2022

The legal framework

If an employee's menopause symptoms are a disability, they can potentially bring the following claims:

- Direct discrimination – treating an employee less favourably because of their disability.
- Discrimination arising from disability – treating an employee unfavourably because of something arising from their disability without a good reason.
- Indirect discrimination – applying a provision, criterion or practice (PCP) that places the employee, and those with that disability, at a disadvantage when compared to someone who is not disabled and where the employer cannot provide a good reason for having the PCP.
- Failure to make reasonable adjustments – a failure to comply with the duty to make reasonable adjustments for an employee whose disability places them at a substantial disadvantage in the workplace.
- Victimisation – treating an employee unfavourably because they bring a claim or complaint of disability discrimination.
- Harassment – subjecting an employee to unwanted conduct that has the purpose or effect of violating the employee's dignity or creating an intimidating, hostile, degrading, humiliating or offensive environment for the employee (and where the employer cannot show that they took all reasonable steps to prevent the conduct from occurring).

Employer's knowledge of menopause as a disability

An employer cannot be liable for direct disability discrimination, discrimination arising from disability or failure to make reasonable adjustments unless it knew, or should have known, about the employee's disability.

This was illustrated in *McMahon v Rothwell and Evans LLP*.[21] Ms McMahon was dismissed for timekeeping problems, taking extended breaks and continued absences. She said that the reason for her timekeeping problems and absences was her menopause symptoms. She brought claims for direct disability discrimination, discrimination arising from disability and failure to make reasonable adjustments. The tribunal held that her menopause symptoms amounted to a disability but did not accept that the employer had knowledge of the disability. Therefore, none of her disability discrimination claims could succeed.

It is a question of fact in each case whether the information disclosed by an employee about their menopause symptoms is sufficient to provide the employer with the knowledge that these symptoms, either in isolation or considered cumulatively, may amount to a disability. Depending on the facts, where an employer has been told that an employee is experiencing menopause, the employee may be able to establish that the employer had constructive, if not actual, knowledge of a disability. The employer should therefore always explore menopause-related issues sensitively with

---

21 ET 2410998/2019

the employee to determine whether further investigation or action is needed.

Duty to make reasonable adjustments for menopause

Where an individual is disabled, their employer is obliged to make reasonable adjustments for them.

The duty to make reasonable adjustments can arise where a disabled person is placed at a substantial disadvantage by any of the following:

- An employer's PCP
- A physical feature of an employer's premises
- An employer's failure to provide an auxiliary aid

In such cases, employers are obliged to do what is reasonable to remove the disadvantage.

Some examples of PCPs that have already been considered by employment tribunals in a menopause context include:

- A requirement to wear a uniform buttoned up to the neck (*Soklova v Humdinger*[22])
- A requirement to work in an environment in which air quality and temperature control were 'below the required standard' (*Sloan v Dumfries and Galloway Health Board*[23]).

---

22 ET 1805866/2020
23 ET 4100022/2020

- A requirement for reasonable attendance levels (*McMahon v Rothwell & Evans LLP* and *Lynskey v Direct Line*[24]).
- A requirement to maintain performance standards (*Lynskey v Direct Line*).

Each person's experience of menopause is individual to them. As a result, the adjustments that might be reasonably required will differ from person to person. The EHRC guidance on menopause in the workplace suggests the following adjustments should be on the radar of employers:

- Providing a quiet or rest area – to assist those handling fatigue and poor concentration
- Providing access to cooling systems or fans – for those experiencing hot flushes
- Relaxing uniform policies or allowing the wearing of loose clothing
- Promoting flexibility in terms of both working time and working from home
- Recording menopause-related absence separately from other absences – to assist those whose symptoms mean that they would be disadvantaged if otherwise subject to unadjusted attendance management procedures

The making of reasonable adjustments is a legal obligation towards disabled employees. However, employers also have a wider duty to protect health and safety and to promote the wellbeing of all of their employees. This duty applies

---

24 ET 1802204/2022

regardless of whether any difficulties they may be facing at work are technically a disability. This book considers this more general issue of adjustments in Chapter 10.

Menopause and disability discrimination: case law examples

In *Davies v Scottish Courts and Tribunals Service*, Ms Davies, a court clerk, advised two court users that they may have drunk water containing her cystitis medication. Ms Davies said that menopause caused her to be confused and forgetful, so she could not remember whether the medication had been in the water. However, after the court users were advised to seek medical advice, it was discovered that the medication had not been in the water.

The employer concluded that Ms Davies had lied about the medication being in the water, and she was therefore dismissed. She brought a successful claim for **discrimination arising from disability**. It was agreed that Ms Davies' menopause symptoms amounted to a disability. The tribunal also acknowledged that Ms Davies' disability caused confusion and forgetfulness, which affected her conduct. The employer argued that Ms Davies' dismissal was not discriminatory, stating that it was a proportionate way to achieve the legitimate aim of having trustworthy staff. Whilst this was a legitimate aim, it was not proportionate to have dismissed Ms Davies without considering the impact of her disability on her conduct. They also should have considered that there were other options, such as a warning, which could have achieved the same aim without being discriminatory.

In *Lynskey v Direct Line*,[25] an employment tribunal held that Direct Line treated Mrs Lynskey unfavourably because of something arising from her disability of menopause and failed to make reasonable adjustments. Mrs Lynskey kept her employer fully informed of her menopause symptoms. They impacted her performance at work. Although Direct Line did make some adjustments and provided additional support and training, the tribunal considered that it should have gone further: Mrs Lynskey should not have been formally performance managed, her targets should have been lowered and a move to a different role considered.

25 ET 1802204/2022 and 1802386/2022

Chapter 6

Menopause and age discrimination

'A dinosaur' – that's what one manager called his 55-year-old employee when her menopause symptoms led to perceived poor performance. Ageist comments like this are not only offensive, but they can also lead to costly legal claims. This 2021 tribunal case[26] confirmed that menopause-related age discrimination is a serious issue, with many women being marginalised just as they reach the peak of their careers.

This chapter explores how age discrimination intersects with menopause and how employers can avoid falling into these legal traps.

Although there are exceptions, women generally experience menopause between the ages of 45 and 55. Age is a relevant factor.

Discrimination issues could arise where those of menopausal or post-menopausal age are treated differently from those in other age groups.

Age discrimination can take different forms:

- **Direct discrimination:** treating an employee less favourably than others because of age without objective justification

26 ET/4107766/19

- **Indirect discrimination:** applying a PCP that disadvantages employees of a particular age group without objective justification
- **Harassment:** subjecting an employee to unwanted conduct related to age which has the purpose or effect of violating the employee's dignity or creating an intimidating, hostile, degrading, humiliating or offensive environment for the employee
- **Victimisation:** treating an employee unfavourably because they have made or intend to make an age discrimination complaint

Potential difficulties where a comparator is required

In both direct and indirect age discrimination, the employee must show that their treatment is unfavourable. They must compare it to that of a real or hypothetical person of a different age group.

People experience menopause and perimenopause at different ages – what is the relevant 'age group' here? The reality is that, although case law does not set the 'age group' of menopausal women, tribunals will likely find that employees going through menopause will, for the most part, fall into a clear 'age group'.

In *Sloan v Dumfries and Galloway Health Board*, the tribunal did not challenge Ms Sloan's assertion that 50-65 was the age range for women undergoing menopause when she sought to compare the disadvantage that women in this 'age group' were placed at when compared with younger members of the workforce.

Difficulties with comparators are possibly why claims for age discrimination arising from menopause are, more often than not, combined with a claim of sex discrimination. The employee is usually alleging that she has been treated unfavourably because she is a woman of menopausal age – two characteristics are involved.

Age discrimination and menopause: case examples

In *Sloan v Dumfries and Galloway Health Board*, Mrs Sloan brought a menopause-related claim for indirect age discrimination. She said that the employer had a rule (a PCP) requiring employees to work in a place where the temperature and air quality were too low. She said this put menopausal employees (which she said were those between the ages of 50 and 65) at a disadvantage compared to younger ones.

The tribunal found that the employer had not operated the alleged PCP. However, even if it had, Mrs Sloan had not shown that cold or low-quality air put older people at a particular disadvantage compared to younger people. Her indirect age discrimination claim was unsuccessful.

In *A v Bonmarche Ltd*,[27] Ms A was going through menopause. She was belittled by her male manager in front of younger staff, who laughed. The manager also called her 'a dinosaur' in front of customers. He unfairly criticised her, linking alleged poor performance to her menopause. She

27 ET/4107766/19

brought a claim for age-related harassment. The tribunal agreed. It ruled that the comments about her menopause were clearly related to her age.

In *Thomas v Bibimoney Global Ltd*,[28] Ms Thomas was Bibimoney's CFO. In a meeting, Ms Thomas highlighted funding issues. She suggested the family sell their shares to her and her partner. After this, she faced mistreatment. The business owner told a colleague she was 'menopausal', implying her behaviour was due to her age. Ms Thomas brought a claim for direct age discrimination and age-related harassment.

The tribunal ruled the employer's comment was direct age discrimination. A younger woman wouldn't have faced this. Although it is possible for direct age discrimination to be justified, Bibimoney did not bring forward any justification. The comment was also age-related harassment. The tribunal accepted Ms Thomas's evidence of how upsetting the comment was to her and accepted that it had amounted to harassment related to age.

These cases were also argued (successfully) as sex discrimination claims, illustrating the intersectional nature of menopause-related discrimination claims.

Summary

Employers need to take care where they have an employee who falls within what might reasonably be regarded as the menopausal 'age group' (accepted to be 50-64 in *Sloan* above

---

28 ET/2204661/22

but which could conceivably be wider than this, especially when incorporating perimenopause). Employers need to:

- Train employees and managers in menopause awareness and set clear standards of appropriate behaviour and language. This reduces the risk of direct age discrimination and harassment claims.
- Ensure that if an employee falling within the menopausal 'age group' takes issue with a PCP operated by the employer, that they take the time to consider whether the PCP places employees in the menopausal 'age group' (and the complaining employee themselves) at a particular disadvantage compared with those of another age group. If it does, they should consider whether the blanket application of the PCP can be justified or whether it should be removed. Issues with sickness absence trigger points and the workplace environment should be looked at with particular sensitivity.

Chapter 7

Menopause and sex discrimination

When Ms Merchant handed her manager a doctor's letter explaining her menopause symptoms, she didn't expect to be dismissed for poor performance shortly after. What followed was a successful sex discrimination claim, where the tribunal found that her manager had dismissed her concerns simply because menopause is 'a female condition'.[29]

This case is just one example of how menopause can lead to sex discrimination. This chapter explores the legal framework and provides guidance on how HR professionals can prevent such discrimination in the workplace.

Direct discrimination

Direct discrimination occurs when an employer treats an employee less favourably than others because of their sex.

In *Merchant v BT plc*,[30] a claim of direct sex discrimination was successful. Ms Merchant was dismissed following a final warning for poor performance. She had already given her manager, Mr Dagless, a letter from her doctor. It explained that she was 'going through menopause which can affect her focus at times'. Mr Dagless chose not to carry out any further

---

29 ET/140135/2011
30 ET/140135/2011

medical investigations of her symptoms before dismissing her.

In tribunal, Mr Dagless accepted that he would normally have referred an employee to occupational health if they raised health issues during a performance-related dismissal. He could not explain why he did not do so this time. The tribunal upheld Ms Merchant's claim for direct sex discrimination. It found that the reason for Mr Dagless's actions was that he did not take menopause seriously because it was a 'female condition' and that he would never have adopted this 'bizarre and irrational approach' with other 'non-female-related conditions'. He had made generalised assumptions about Ms Merchant's condition based on what he had seen his wife experience and whatever his HR manager had told him. The making of these assumptions was less favourable treatment than a male comparator would have experienced.

Harassment

Harassment under the EqA 2010 occurs when an employer subjects an employee to unwanted conduct related to sex that has the purpose or effect of violating the employee's dignity or creating an intimidating, hostile, degrading, humiliating or offensive environment for the employee.

Negative workplace attitudes to menopause can leave employers at risk of sex-related harassment claims. In *Anderson (or Farquharson) v Thistle Marine (Peterhead) Ltd and others*,[31] a Scottish case, an employment tribunal found, perhaps unsurprisingly, that the employer's derogatory comments

31 ET/4101775/2023

about menopause ('Menopause, menopause, a'biddy f**king gets it, just get on wi' it, that's your excuse for everything.') amounted to harassment on the grounds of sex.

In *Best v Embark on Raw Ltd*[32], the employment tribunal found that the claimant, Mrs Best, had suffered sex-related harassment. Her boss, Mr Fletcher, directly asked her whether she was menopausal. The tribunal held that this invaded her privacy and tactlessly broached a highly sensitive topic for her when she had made it clear she did not wish to have any such discussion.

However, if comments are made to support the employee, even if they seem patronising, they may not be considered harassment. In *Newbould v Commissioner of Police of the Metropolis*,[33] Mrs Newbould brought claims for sex-related harassment. She alleged that a male manager, DCI McPherson, belittled her by saying she was probably getting upset about things because of her hormonal state.

The employment tribunal dismissed the claims. Mrs Newbould had herself told DCI McPherson that she was getting upset about minor issues because of menopause, and DCI McPherson had been trying to explore this with her and show empathy. His behaviour may have come across to Mrs Newbould as patronising, but it was not reasonable to consider it harassment. This case is a clear reminder of the importance of management training in this area – something explored in more detail in Chapter 11 and Chapter 12.

32 ET/3202006/2020
33 ET/2205178/2018

Indirect discrimination

Indirect sex discrimination occurs when an employer applies a PCP that disadvantages employees of a particular sex without objective justification.

In *Sokolova v Humdinger Ltd*, Mrs Sokolova was employed in a nut factory. She complained that the employer's PCP of keeping overalls buttoned to the neck worsened her menopausal hot flushes. Humdinger said it could not relax the uniform rule but that it could (and subsequently did) provide fans for staff. However, these fans were available on a 'first come, first served' basis and were usually taken before Mrs Sokolova arrived at work. After her dismissal, she brought a claim for indirect sex discrimination.

The tribunal accepted that hot flushes are a symptom of menopause and that menopause applies to women. There was no evidence before the tribunal to suggest that there are conditions which generate heat intolerances which only apply to men. Therefore, the PCP of having uniforms buttoned up to the neck put women at a substantial disadvantage and Mrs Sokolova was put to that disadvantage.

However, there was a legitimate aim in the PCP (to avoid contamination of food), and the wearing of overalls was appropriate to achieve the aim. In relation to proportionality, it was not practicable for Humdinger to disapply the PCP. Therefore, the PCP was not indirectly discriminatory on the grounds of sex.

Summary

Although there are exceptions, menopause is a female experience. This means that, wherever employers have menopause issues in the workplace, a risk of sex discrimination claims is in play.

Chapter 8

Menopause and gender reassignment

It is important that workplaces do not pigeonhole menopause as an exclusively 'female' issue. Menopause support should be inclusive. Employers should provide the same support to any employee experiencing symptoms.

Menopause impacts anyone who has a menstrual cycle, including some trans men and non-binary people. For those undergoing gender reassignment, medical treatments or surgeries can induce menopause. So, what happens when an employee experiencing menopause symptoms doesn't fit the traditional gender mould?

This chapter explores the intersection of menopause and gender reassignment. It covers how employers can ensure their workplace policies are inclusive, providing support to all employees experiencing menopause – regardless of their gender identity – and how the legal landscape is evolving to protect trans employees from discrimination in this context.

Can trans employees claim sex discrimination?

It is interesting to consider what claim a trans employee could bring if they felt that they were being treated unfavourably in some way by their employer in relation to menopause.

The legal position on sex discrimination in this context is currently in a state of flux. In *For Women Scotland Ltd v Scottish Ministers*,[34] the Inner House of the Court of Session held that the EqA 2010 definition of 'woman' must include trans women with a gender recognition certificate (GRC), noting that section 9(1) of the *Gender Recognition Act 2004* (GRA 2004) states that the gender of a person with a GRC becomes 'for all purposes' that of their acquired gender. Applying *For Women Scotland*, a trans man with a GRC, whose legal sex under the GRA 2004 is male, would be a man under the EqA 2010. This would mean that, if they experienced menopause symptoms, they could not bring a menopause-related direct or indirect sex discrimination claim as a woman.

By contrast, a trans woman who has a GRC and who is experiencing menopause symptoms (something which can arise from fluctuating levels of oestrogen associated with hormone replacement therapy) could bring a menopause-related direct or indirect sex discrimination claim under the EqA 2010 as a woman.

The current position is anomalous. The Equality and Human Rights Commission has recently issued guidance to the effect that 'sex' under the EqA 2010 should refer to biological sex. If legislative change is made to give effect to this guidance, then the decision in *For Women Scotland* would no longer stand. A trans man **would** be able to bring a sex discrimination claim in relation to menopause issues.

34 [2023] CSIH 37

Gender reassignment discrimination

Those who are proposing to undergo, are undergoing or have undergone sex reassignment are protected from discrimination. This is under the protected characteristic of gender reassignment.

The EHRC, in its guidance on gender reassignment discrimination,[35] states that:

> *"To be protected from gender reassignment discrimination, you do not need to have undergone any medical treatment or surgery to change from your birth sex to your preferred gender.*
>
> *You can be at any stage in the transition process, from proposing to reassign your sex, undergoing a process of reassignment, or having completed it. It does not matter whether or not you have applied for or obtained a Gender Recognition Certificate, which is the document that confirms the change of a person's legal sex."*

Under the EqA 2010, it is possible for an individual to bring the following claims related to the protected characteristic of gender reassignment:

- Direct discrimination
- Less favourable treatment because of absence from work for gender reassignment
- Indirect discrimination
- Harassment
- Victimisation

35 https://www.equalityhumanrights.com/equality/equality-act-2010/your-rights-under-equality-act-2010/gender-reassignment-discrimination

If, for example, an employer treats an individual with the protected characteristic of gender reassignment and who is experiencing menopause symptoms less favourably than a woman experiencing menopause symptoms, then this could amount to direct gender reassignment discrimination.

The importance of confidentiality

There are additional factors for employers to consider when an employee protected by the characteristic of gender reassignment raises menopause issues. Some individuals may not have shared their gender identity in the workplace. Employers must be careful to respect confidentiality obligations. It can be a criminal offence for an employer who finds out information about a person's gender identity to share that information more widely (section 22 of the GRA 2004).

Chapter 9

Menopause and unfair dismissal

As a general rule, employers need a fair reason to dismiss an employee. They must also act fairly in doing so. (Note: until Autumn 2026, this chapter will not apply to employees with less than two years' employment.)

If menopause symptoms are an active issue, then employers are expected to take them into account when considering whether it would be reasonable to dismiss.

There is clear scope for menopause to be a relevant factor in both conduct and performance dismissals – and there are tribunal cases covering both of these areas.

Menopause and misconduct dismissals

Menopause-related unfair dismissal claims often concern employees who were dismissed for misconduct. As in all misconduct dismissals, an employer must show that it carried out a reasonable investigation before the dismissal (*British Home Stores v Burchell*[36]). When an employee being disciplined is experiencing menopause and argues that this affected or caused their behaviour, it is likely to be unfair for

36 [1978] IRLR 379

the employer to dismiss without investigating whether this could be the case.

In *Davies v Scottish Courts and Tribunals Service*, the employer dismissed Ms Davies after she mistakenly informed two court users that they may have drunk water containing her cystitis medication. Ms Davies' claim for unfair dismissal was upheld. The health and safety investigation triggered by the incident said she had lied about the medication being in the water. This report tainted the rest of the dismissal process, which amounted to a fundamental flaw in the process. It meant that the employer failed to listen to what Ms Davies was saying. For example, the disciplinary and appeal hearing chairs simply rejected her explanation that she had been confused and made a mistake about the medication being in the water. They focused on the health and safety report's conclusion, which was that she had lied about it. There were no reasonable grounds for the conclusion that Ms Davies had lied.

The employer had also failed to consider Ms Davies' medical condition. It was aware that she could be affected by memory loss and confusion but ignored her explanation that this may have caused her to act as she had. The employer's decision to dismiss was outside the range of reasonable responses.

In *Krolik v Youngs Seafood Ltd*,[37] Ms Krolik was dismissed after angrily disrupting a meeting in which she was told that she would have to take holiday at a time specified by Youngs. She was accused of having attended work under the influence of alcohol.

---

37 ET 4107394/2020

During her disciplinary hearing, she broke down and explained that she had an alcohol problem that had been made worse by family issues and menopause. She denied that she had been drunk at work but explained that 'her rage was not good' and suggested this was why she had disrupted the meeting. The employer did not ask Ms Krolik any further questions about her health condition.

The tribunal found that the dismissal was unfair because the employer failed to carry out a reasonable investigation. Although Ms Krolik had indicated that she believed menopause was affecting her emotions at work, the employer did not investigate this further and did not refer her to occupational health about her menopause or alcohol issues. The decision to dismiss was therefore outside the range of reasonable responses.

However, where a tribunal finds that a misconduct dismissal is unfair because the employer has failed to consider menopause, the employer may be able to argue that either:

- A deduction should apply to reduce the compensation (in some cases to zero) because the dismissal would have occurred anyway. (This happened in *Matthews v Bircham Dyson Bell.*[38])
- Compensation should be reduced because of the employee's contributory fault.

38 ET 2208036/2016

Menopause and capability dismissals

If an employer is considering a capability dismissal because of an employee's poor performance, but the employee argues that menopause has affected their performance, it is likely to be unfair for the employer to dismiss without first having investigated what effect menopause may have had.

In *Merchant v BT*, the claimant's dismissal for poor performance was found to be unfair. It was held that although BT genuinely believed Ms Merchant was incompetent, there were no reasonable grounds for this belief. She had been employed for 24 years with no serious performance concerns. She had given her manager a letter from her doctor explaining that menopause may have affected her performance, but her manager had failed to properly investigate this. Instead, he improperly relied on the menopause experiences of his wife and HR manager as giving him sufficient knowledge of the health condition.

Menopause and constructive dismissal

A constructive dismissal occurs when an employee resigns in response to the employer's fundamental breach of the employment contract. The breach relied upon is the implied term of trust and confidence. If an employer handles an employee's menopause symptoms insensitively or inappropriately, then this could, in principle, amount to a breach of trust and confidence. An employee facing such treatment would be entitled to resign and claim constructive unfair dismissal.

This was illustrated in *Johnson v Bronzeshield Lifting Limited*.[39] In this case, the claimant made a flexible working request. She gave two reasons for the request: to assist with caring for her elderly parents and to help with 'menopause issues'. Her manager refused the request and completely ignored what she had said about menopause. The claimant resigned and claimed constructive dismissal. Her claim was successful. The tribunal found that by failing to consider the impact of the claimant's menopause, the respondent had breached the implied term of trust and confidence.

Although the employee's claim was unsuccessful on the facts (she was found to have delayed too long before resigning), *Lynskey v Direct Line* also supports this position. In this case, the tribunal considered that the following actions of Direct Line, who were aware of Mrs Lynskey's menopause symptoms, breached the implied term of trust and confidence by:

- Giving Mrs Lynskey an annual appraisal rating of 'need for improvement', which resulted in a lack of pay rise and was imposed without any discussion or recognition of Mrs Lynskey's disability
- Giving Mrs Lynskey a written warning
- Withdrawing discretionary sick pay before the end of Mrs Lynskey's entitlement.

39 ET 2303313/2022

Summary

Failing to take account of the impact of menopause symptoms when dismissing an employee risks the dismissal being unfair.

Given that menopause can be linked to protected characteristics such as sex, age and disability, employers also risk the dismissal being found to be discriminatory. This brings the additional financial risk factor of an injury to feelings award into play. Compensation for discriminatory dismissals is potentially unlimited.

Whenever menopause is a possible factor in behaviour or performance issues, the employer needs to be able to demonstrate that it has considered any appropriate adjustments to its normal processes and additional support.

Disciplinary officers need to be trained and educated on menopause. Employers cannot have disciplinary officers like the one in *Merchant v BT*, relying on what others have told them about menopause symptoms as the basis for any action taken.

Chapter 10

Making adjustments for menopause

Imagine being in a meeting, your mind suddenly going blank and being unable to focus. You feel a hot flush rising, and all you want is a few minutes to gather yourself. Now imagine being in an office where you can't adjust the temperature, step outside for air or take a brief break. For many employees experiencing menopause, this is a daily reality. But small changes – like a fan at a desk or flexible work hours – could make all the difference.

This chapter explores the practical adjustments employers can make to create a menopause-friendly environment.

In severe cases, menopause may amount to a disability. In these circumstances, an employer is under a legal obligation to make reasonable adjustments (see Chapter 5).

But, even if menopause is not a disability, an employer has a duty to protect health and safety. This duty comes from the *Management of Health and Safety at Work Regulations 1999*. Employers must assess the risks to the health and safety of employees at work. Risk assessments should consider the specific needs of those experiencing menopause to make sure that symptoms aren't made worse by the working environment.

Acas guidance[40] suggests that a menopause risk assessment could include:

- The temperature and ventilation of the workplace
- The material and fit of the business's uniform and whether it might make staff going through menopause feel too hot or cause them discomfort
- Whether there is somewhere suitable for staff to rest, if necessary – for example, a quiet room
- Whether toilet facilities are easily accessible
- Whether cold drinking water is available
- Whether managers have been trained on health and safety issues relating to menopause

An employer should explore the possibility of making an adjustment to working conditions to respond to menopause-specific risks. Acas and the EHRC give the following examples of adjustments that employers could make, where possible and practical:

- Promoting flexibility
- Being flexible about start and finish times
- Changing shift patterns
- Allowing breaks when needed
- Providing a private area or quiet room in which to rest
- Allowing home working

40 https://www.acas.org.uk/menopause-at-work/supporting-staff-through-the-menopause

- Allowing time off
- Making changes to duties
- Providing cooling systems or fans
- Allowing individuals control over their working environment by, for example, having a desk next to an opening window or providing a fan
- Relaxing uniform policies or allowing cooler clothing to be worn

While physical adjustments (such as managing hot flushes or fatigue) are crucial, employers should prioritise mental health support on an equal footing. Psychological symptoms may not be as visible as physical ones but can be just as impactful. Mental health should be included in any menopause risk assessment just as physical issues are.

A 2023 survey of 2,000 workers by inclusive design company Motionspot[41] suggested that the most helpful workplace features for those experiencing issues with menstruation and menopause are fresh air, comfortable desk seating, natural light, a private room, temperature-controlled spaces and focus rooms with fewer distractions.

Any adjustments agreed with an individual should be recorded in writing. The employer should ensure that there are follow-up discussions to make sure the adjustments remain appropriate over time.

---

41 https://workinmind.org/2023/08/24/research-menopause-menstration-motionspot

Managing menopause-related sickness and performance issues

Since menopause is a health condition, staff may need time off to manage their symptoms. Acas and the EHRC suggest that employers should record menopause-related absences separately. This is because it may be discriminatory to count them as part of a person's overall attendance record or to discipline them for it. Additionally, though not legally required, Acas suggests that it is good practice for employers to allow employees time off to attend medical appointments related to menopause.

Where menopause affects an individual's performance at work, case law shows that it could sometimes be unfair or discriminatory to penalise the employee. The scale of the problem is illustrated in the data gathered by Motionspot in its survey. It found that 43% of respondents had brain fog due to menopause or perimenopause and that 65% struggled with concentration. It is not hard to see how issues like these could find themselves framed (perhaps inappropriately) as performance issues.

Whenever an employee says that menopause has affected their performance, their employer should bear in mind its obligation to consider adjustments.

Chapter 11

Creating a menopause-friendly workplace

When Severn Trent Water introduced its menopause policy in 2018, it marked the start of a cultural shift.[42] Today, Severn Trent Water is seen as a leader in menopause-friendly workplaces, offering workshops, menopause guides and manager training.[43]

This chapter provides concrete steps to help businesses become more menopause-friendly, improving both employee wellbeing and business outcomes.

Implement a menopause policy

A menopause policy ensures that staff know where to find information about the support that is available to them when experiencing menopause. Provided the policy is well advertised and easily accessible, it can serve as a first port of call when a menopause-related issue occurs. A menopause policy template is available at Appendix 1.

42 https://www.wellbeingofwomen.org.uk/what-we-do/campaigns/menopause-stories/the-menopause-is-absolutely-something-we-should-be-talking-about

43 https://menopauseintheworkplace.co.uk/articles/menopause-severn-trent

Acas guidance[44] suggests that a menopause policy can help everyone in a business to understand what menopause is, what the symptoms are and that it affects everyone differently. It can also:

- Explain what training is provided to managers, supervisors and team leaders
- Explain who the business's point of contact is for queries related to menopause
- Show how the business is open and trained to talk and listen sensitively about menopause
- Include the employer's commitment to support its diverse workforce and to prevent discrimination

Obtain independent accreditation

Employers could also consider signing up to the Menopause Workplace Pledge. By signing the pledge, employers recognise that menopause can be a workplace issue for which employees need support. Signatories commit to open, positive and respectful workplace dialogue about menopause, and to taking active steps to support employees affected by menopause and informing them of the support offered.

There are other accreditations available, such as the 'Menopause Friendly' badge, which is issued by Menopause Friendly, an independent body working to make every workplace menopause friendly.

44 https://www.acas.org.uk/menopause-at-work

Encourage open conversations

Employers should encourage an environment in which staff can have open conversations about menopause. This helps individuals who are experiencing menopause to come forward when an issue arises.

Acas guidance suggests that all managers should be trained in how to talk about menopause. To help remove the taboo around menopause issues, managers should discuss menopause with all staff alongside other diversity and health and wellbeing topics. Managers must bear in mind that it may not always be obvious who is experiencing menopause symptoms. Managers should hold regular check-ins, where they ask open-ended questions such as, "How are you feeling, and is there anything that could help support you right now?" This enables employees to share health struggles (including mental health struggles) more easily.

On the same theme, the EHRC guidance[45] says that open conversations about menopause should involve all workers, not just management, to encourage a culture where workers feel able to talk about their symptoms and request workplace adjustments. It suggests training, lunch and learn sessions, and other opportunities for workers to discuss their experiences and get support, such as staff networks, as well as sending regular reminders of the support available to workers and holding confidential meetings with managers to discuss any issues.

45 https://www.equalityhumanrights.com/guidance/menopause-workplace-guidance-employers

Employees may feel uncomfortable talking about menopause with their direct manager. It can therefore be helpful to have an alternative point of contact within the business (for example, a member of HR or a menopause champion) who is also trained to deal with menopause-related issues.

Offer access to mental health services

Menopause symptoms are often psychological as well as physical. Support for mental health needs to be prioritised. This can be done in a number of ways, including:

- Signposting access to external support, such as employee assistance programmes (EAPs), which offer confidential access to counselling services where employees can seek help for menopause-related mental health issues.
- Training selected employees as mental health first aiders to provide immediate, informed support to those struggling with anxiety or depression due to menopause. These employees could work alongside any appointed menopause champion.

Promote flexible working

Flexible working arrangements can reduce stress and anxiety, allowing employees the autonomy to manage their mental health.

Employers should make clear that seeking flexibility is an option available to assist those going through menopause.

Provide cognitive support mechanisms

For employees suffering from 'brain fog,' simple adjustments, such as clearer communication and breaking down tasks, can make a big difference.

Adopting a 'bitesize' approach to communication and tasks might benefit the workforce as a whole. Employers should review the apps and products available and ensure that productivity tools, like note-taking apps, reminders and task organisers, are available to employees. They can help employees manage cognitive symptoms.

Appoint a menopause champion

Acas suggests appointing a workplace menopause champion to give staff an alternative point of contact if they need advice on menopause-related issues or if they are not comfortable talking to their manager. A workplace menopause champion may also be able to support the employer in other ways, for example, by running educational workshops or checking that health and safety risk assessments cover menopause-related issues.

Undertake a workplace audit

Employers know their businesses best. They should take a look at the workplace environment and culture through the eyes of a menopausal employee. Where are the key areas of concern? They should undertake a workplace audit, take action where problems are highlighted and repeat the audit at regular intervals to quickly capture any new problem areas that might arise.

The audit process should also include a review of past performance. What has the business done when employees have raised menopause symptoms in the past? What learning can be put in place from this? What could've been done better?

Make use of confidential surveys and feedback loops

Employers can get a more complete understanding of the difficulties faced by those experiencing menopause symptoms in the workplace if they gather information confidentially.

For example, a confidential survey might highlight an issue with constricting uniform. A small relaxation in uniform policy to allow the wearing of loose-fitting clothes could dramatically increase the levels of comfort of those struggling with hot flushes. There will be a knock-on positive effect on productivity, and employees will feel 'heard' – a win-win.

Feedback loops can be used to make sure that employers don't treat action to support menopause in the workplace as a 'once and done' issue. Within a business, encouraging regular, two-way communication between managers and employees helps to keep the issue live and enable quick action to eliminate new issues and frustrations as they arise.

Chapter 12

How to have workplace conversations about menopause

Imagine walking into work one day, feeling utterly drained after another sleepless night and plagued by hot flushes, anxiety and brain fog – yet you're expected to perform at your best. Now imagine trying to explain that to your manager, knowing they may not understand or support you. This is the reality for countless women in workplaces where menopause remains a taboo topic.

Or imagine you are a manager. You have a previously well-performing employee whose concentration and attention have fallen off a cliff. You think that menopause might be behind the drop, but you don't know how to start the conversation.

What if it doesn't have to be this way? What if open conversations about menopause were as routine as discussing flexible working arrangements?

This chapter explores how employers can create a workplace where menopause is openly discussed, support is easily accessible and all employees feel respected and valued.

When considering 'workplace conversations' it is important to consider two distinct issues:

1. How can employers create a workplace environment where menopause is talked about openly and where colleagues are supportive of, and respectful to, each other?
2. How can an employer hold supportive one-to-one discussions with:
   a. Employees who have revealed that they are menopausal?
   b. Those who the employer believes may be menopausal and whose conduct or performance is suffering, but who have not revealed their condition?

Arguably, if an employer is able to hit the ground running on the first of these, the second becomes much easier. An open and supportive workplace is likely to create an atmosphere where employees feel safe and supported and can discuss their health.

Making menopause an open workplace topic for discussion

A workplace where menopause is not an open topic for discussion is a workplace open to significant risk. In *Johnson v Bronzeshield Lifting Limited*,[46] the claimant succeeded in a claim of direct disability discrimination after the respondent completely ignored her menopause issues when considering a flexible working request. In evidence, the manager handling the request said he had ignored it because he did not understand it and wouldn't be able to.

46 ET/2302213/2022

The EHRC guidance suggests that it is key to get all employees involved in conversations about menopause, not just management. They suggest the following tools:

- Training for all employees to increase knowledge, understanding and empathy
- Lunch and learn sessions
- Opportunities for women to discuss their experiences
- Staff networks and other 'safe spaces'
- Creation of a menopause policy signposting support available
- Asking staff to become 'menopause champions' to support their department or business area with menopause issues

Having the conversation

Scenario 1: An employee discloses they are going through menopause

When an employee tells their employer they are experiencing menopause, the initial response should be supportive and empathetic. The employer should acknowledge the disclosure positively, thanking the employee for their openness and trust. For example, by saying:

"Thank you for sharing this with me. I appreciate how personal this is, and I want to make sure we support you effectively."

The employer should get the employee's agreement if it thinks it might need to discuss the employee's disclosure more widely (for example, with HR or facilities). Information relating to health is sensitive personal data, and the employee's consent is generally required to disclose it.

- **Discuss specific needs** – Each individual's experience with menopause is unique. Employers should engage in a discussion about the employee's specific symptoms and how these might affect their work. Employers should ask open-ended questions to understand the employee's needs, such as:

  "What kind of adjustments or support do you think might help you at work during this time?"

- **Implement reasonable adjustments** – Employers should consider reasonable adjustments (see Chapter 5 and Chapter 10). They should ensure that any adjustments comply with health and safety standards and respect the employee's privacy and dignity.

- **Provide access to resources** – Employers should offer resources that might help the employee manage their symptoms more effectively, such as occupational health services, counselling or information about relevant support groups. Employers should ensure that all employees are aware of these resources through regular communications.

- **Review regularly** – Menopausal symptoms can change over time, so it's crucial that employers have regular check-ins with the employee to revisit and adjust the support and adjustments provided.

Scenario 2: An employer suspects an employee may be going through menopause

There may be circumstances where a supportive employer will want to know whether or not an employee is menopausal. For example, if there are conduct or performance issues which are otherwise out of character, or the employee is struggling in the workplace.

It is not unlawful for an employer to ask an employee whether they are going through menopause. However, how an employer goes about asking the question is crucially important. In *Beasley v Rainbow Trust*,[47] the question was asked by a female line manager who was herself going through menopause. When the employee answered in the negative, the question was not asked again. The employer did not press the point. This, the tribunal said, was important. The issue is case-specific.

- **Exercise caution** – If you suspect an employee is going through menopause but they have not raised it themselves, approach the topic with extreme caution. It is sensitive personal information and broaching it directly could be seen as intrusive and could potentially lead to accusations of discrimination.
- **Focus on work performance** – Instead of directly mentioning menopause, frame any discussion around work performance and general wellbeing. This can open a conversation without making assumptions about health. Use phrases like:

47 ET/2502593/2019 and ET/2501428/2020

"I've noticed some changes in your [specify behaviour such as 'attendance' or 'engagement with work'], and I wanted to check in to see if there's anything you need or anything we can do to support you better."

"I want to make sure you feel supported at work. If there are adjustments or resources that could help you or improve your work experience, please let me know."

- **Provide training and awareness** – Provide training for managers on how to handle sensitive health discussions appropriately. Raising awareness about menopause as a normal part of life can reduce stigma and make these conversations less daunting for both parties.
- **Offer general support** – Rather than asking directly, ensure that all staff are aware of the support available for a range of health issues, including menopause. This can be communicated through staff handbooks, HR policies and health and wellness programmes.

Summary

Where it is necessary to speak to staff experiencing menopause (or who may be experiencing menopause) about their condition, Acas explains that these conversations should be confidential and held in private.[48] The manager (or other point of contact) should let the employee disclose only as much information as they are comfortable to and should not share information about the

48 https://www.acas.org.uk/menopause-at-work/talking-with-staff-about-the-menopause

employee's condition without their permission. The manager should keep a written record of the conversation. This advice applies both where the employer knows that the employee is menopausal and where the employer is seeking to establish if the employee is.

Ultimately, everything comes back to workplace culture. If you have an open and supportive workplace culture, then these difficult conversations are so much easier. They become part of the everyday work experience. All employees feel safe to bring their true selves (brain fog, hot flushes and all!) to work.

Chapter 13
Case studies showcasing how different businesses currently manage menopause at work

When employers are looking to implement menopause support in the workplace, they can take inspiration from other businesses and the approach they have taken. This chapter sets out some case studies that show how real businesses in the UK tackle this issue.

Case study 1: University of Greenwich

The EHRC guidance includes an interview with the University of Greenwich, in which they explain how they support employees through menopause. Measures include:

- Upskilling their menopause project team so that they can provide in-house menopause training three times a year to managers and colleagues
- Appointing menopause champions in every faculty and directorate to talk with colleagues experiencing menopause and signpost available support
- Including a short video on menopause in their induction process to make clear to new starters that it is okay to talk about menopause at work

The University found that these steps fostered a culture of openness about menopause that has had a dramatic impact. An employee losing their train of thought when speaking in a meeting felt comfortable and supported in saying, 'I'm just having a menopause moment'. Her explanation was supported and, most importantly, understood.

Case study 2: Severn Trent Water

Severn Trent Water has emerged as a leader in supporting menopausal employees. It even reaches out to other businesses to support them in introducing their own menopause support in the workplace. Steps taken include:

- Introducing a menopause policy as early as 2018
- Hosting an annual workshop for employees at all levels
- Conducting menopause awareness sessions for all employees of all ages
- Having guides to support the needs of women tailored to each stage of the menopause process – formulated with input from staff

Case study 3: Tesco

Tesco was held up as an example by the Government, which reported in 2023[49] that Tesco has updated its sickness policy so that if colleagues take time off due to menopause-related

49 https://assets.publishing.service.gov.uk/media/653111700b5392000da929c4/no-time-to-step-back-menopause-champion.pdf

symptoms, the absence is not counted as a period of absence under the company's sickness absence policy.

Tesco has introduced a new menopause-friendly uniform, a virtual networking group on menopause, signed the Menopause Workplace Pledge and released a menopause guide for colleagues.

Case study 4: What not to do – Avanti West Coast

The businesses featured so far in this chapter have hit the ground running in terms of providing menopause support in the workplace. If you are just embarking on your business's journey and these stories leave you feeling a little inadequate, then don't lose heart. For every 'best practice' example there is always an example of a business that has got it spectacularly wrong. Step forward Avanti West Coast!

Avanti West Coast's latest attempt to support employees going through menopause resulted in a bit of an 'own goal' and a whole heap of bad press![50] Someone at Avanti thought it was a good idea to hand out a goodie bag to female employees containing 'gimmick' menopause-related gifts. Avanti confirmed that it had given staff a bag filled with 'gifts' including a jelly baby 'in case you feel like biting someone's head off', a paper clip 'to help you keep it all together', a tissue 'if you're feeling a bit emotional' and a pencil 'to write down the things you might forget'. Other items included a fan 'handy for the hot sweats'.

50 https://www.theguardian.com/society/2024/feb/16/unions-criticise-demeaning-gift-bag-for-menopausal-staff-at-avanti-west-coast

The Aslef train drivers' union shared a photo of the list and wrote on X:

"Avanti, the menopause is debilitating for some women, it's not a joke … Rather than handing out insulting gimmicks to female employees, you'd be better placed developing workplace policies and procedures that value and support perimenopausal and menopausal women!"

It is a reminder, if one is needed, that employers should think very carefully about the messages their actions send out and be aware of the full range of employee experience when dealing with menopause.

Chapter 14

The future for menopause in the workplace

What might the future look like for menopause in the workplace? This final chapter considers several sources that indicate the direction of travel.

Political policy

On World Menopause Day (18 October) 2023, an all-parliamentary group published a Manifesto for Menopause, calling on all political parties to commit to a seven-point programme of reform.[51] The employment aspects of the manifesto included:

- Requiring that employers with over 250 employees produce a menopause action plan to support employees in the workplace
- Providing guidance to small and medium-sized enterprises about how to handle menopause issues in the workplace

51 https://menopause-appg.co.uk/wp-content/uploads/2023/10/APPG-Menopause-Manifesto-for-Menopause.pdf

- Introducing tax incentives to encourage employers to incorporate menopause support into occupational health provision

The first of these suggestions for reform has been picked up by the government. Clause 26 of the *Employment Rights Bill* (published in October 2024) proposes to introduce a requirement for businesses with at least 250 employees to develop and publish a 'menopause action plan'. The plan would need to demonstrate how the business supports employees going through menopause. Prior to the publication of the Bill, Deputy Prime Minister Angela Rayner said:

"Employers will be required to submit their plans annually to the existing government portal used for gender pay gap reporting."

The Bill explains that regulations will be published in due course to make provisions about:

- The content of a plan
- The form and manner in which a plan or information is to be published
- When and how frequently a plan or information is to be published or revised
- Requirements for senior approval before a plan or information is published

Menopause action plans will not become mandatory until 2026 at the earliest. However, employers might decide to develop one now and may wish to include:

- How they will raise menopause awareness in the workplace

- Details of any relevant policies they have in place (or plans for introducing/revising them), including any specific menopause policy and flexible working policy
- How they will train managers to support those going through menopause
- Details of any wellbeing policies and access to any external or internal wellness and support programmes
- Reasonable adjustments they may be able to consider
- Environmental adjustments they may be able to make to the workplace environment

The Role of the media, think tanks and advocacy groups

The media, think tanks and advocacy groups have been instrumental in pushing menopause up the agenda.

TV presenter Davina McCall is one of several high-profile advocates calling for more candid discourse on menopause. In America, actress Naomi Watts launched a new wellness brand that focuses on perimenopause and menopause with biotech company Amyris, joining a growing number of female entrepreneurs developing products aimed at alleviating the array of symptoms menopausal women can face.

The Women and Equalities Committee has been vocal about menopause being an issue of equality in the workplace, recommending that it be treated with the same seriousness as other health conditions that affect job performance and satisfaction.

Summary

The trajectory for menopause in the workplace in the UK is one of progressive change and growing recognition. Political pledges, along with the efforts of think tanks and the proactive measures taken by businesses, point towards a future where menopause is openly discussed and effectively supported in professional settings.

As legislation catches up with societal shifts, and as more businesses recognise the benefits of supporting menopausal employees, the workplace will become a more welcoming space for everyone, irrespective of their life stage. This transition will, in turn, reduce employers' exposure to legal risks associated with menopause and the workplace.

Appendix 1
Menopause Policy template

1. Introduction

1.1. Menopause is something that we are all affected by, either directly or indirectly. We want you to understand what menopause is and how it might affect people. We want to remove any stigma associated with menopause. This is the best way of making sure that everyone impacted by it feels supported and understood.

1.2. This Policy:

a. Sets out what menopause is

b. Explains how it might affect people, both directly and indirectly

c. Provides a clear explanation of the support networks in place across our business to help those who may need support on this issue

d. Sets out expected conduct and behaviour towards colleagues who are affected, directly or indirectly, by menopause

1.3. Please note that this Policy does not form part of your contract with us. We reserve the right to amend or remove this Policy.

1.4. This Policy applies to all employees, contractors, agency workers, casual workers, interns and volunteers working for us.

2. What is menopause?

2.1. Menopause occurs when a woman stops having menstrual periods. It is triggered by a reduction in the production of the hormone oestrogen. Menopause usually occurs between 45 and 55 years old. However, the timing and symptoms are different for everyone.

2.2. It's not only those who identify as women who will experience menopause. Some transgender men, non-binary people and intersex people or people with variations in sex characteristics may also experience menopause. In this Policy, reference to a specific gender should be taken to include all genders.

2.3. Menopause is split into perimenopause and postmenopause. Perimenopause marks the start of menopausal symptoms and may last several years. Postmenopause is the time after a woman experiences her last period.

3. What are the common symptoms of menopause?

3.1. Menopause affects each person differently. Three out of four women will have symptoms, and one out of four women will have severe symptoms. Symptoms are both physical and psychological in nature and can change over time.

3.2. Common symptoms include:

- Hot flushes
- Headaches
- Poor concentration
- Dry eyes
- Anxiety
- Low mood
- Lack of confidence
- Panic attacks
- Poor sleep
- Weight gain
- Fatigue
- Poor memory
- Joint and muscle pain

4. The role of managers

4.1. We are committed to supporting you through menopause. This process starts with creating an environment where discussion about menopause isn't taboo – it is out in the open and understood. We do not want our employees to feel embarrassed or awkward.

4.2. For managers, recognising the symptoms of menopause is vital to treating an affected employee fairly. It can explain certain behaviours that might otherwise be put down to a bad attitude or poor performance.

4.3. [We will give managers specific training in handling all menopause-related issues sensitively and with confidence. This is not just about legal compliance; good support at work leads to happier and better-performing employees who have valuable skills and experience.] [If you are a manager and think that someone who reports to you may be going through menopause and it is affecting their performance, if you are not sure what to do, please contact [*insert relevant name*].] Women who don't get the right support can lose confidence in their ability to do their jobs (some may even decide to leave) and may find that their mental health suffers.

5. **Support through menopause**

5.1. We know that menopause is a very personal matter, so we will not raise it with you even if we think you are displaying symptoms. We might ask how you are, in general terms. You can then decide whether to talk to us about menopause or not. We encourage you to do so because we want to support you.

5.2. We have a four-step procedure that applies to discussions around menopause and the action we'll take.

5.3. <u>Step 1</u>

a. You could start by speaking with your GP or medical specialist about your menopause-related concerns.

b. You could also talk to [*insert relevant person or department*], or you could go straight to your [*line manager*] (see Step 2) if you feel comfortable doing that.

5.4. <u>Step 2</u>

a. Meet with your [*line manager*]. [All managers have been trained in understanding and helping employees through menopause.] You should expect to be able to have a private, friendly, honest and constructive conversation.

b. We will discuss with you ideas that could make things easier for you. Adjustments will depend on different factors, but things you could ask us to consider include:

- Modifying your [uniform] [dress code]
- Installing a water cooler
- Giving you a desk fan
- Making a room available for rest
- Allowing you more frequent breaks
- Extending deadlines
- Agreeing a flexible working arrangement (e.g. a change in working hours or homeworking)
- Altering some aspects of your duties

c. Your conversation with your [*line manager*] will be confidential. They will probably need to discuss issues and possible solutions with others, including [*HR*] [*other managers*] [*your GP*] [*a company doctor*] [*occupational health*]. Those people are subject to duties of confidentiality.

d. We will work hard to balance your needs with those of your colleagues; however, on occasions, we may not be able to find a solution that works for everyone.

e. We will keep notes of the things we discuss and will comply with our data protection responsibilities in respect of the information that passes between us, in line with our [*Data Protection Policy*].

f. After your initial meeting with your [*line manager*], and periodically after that, we may carry out health and safety risk assessments and/or seek advice from occupational health.

5.5. Step 3

a. Taking account of any specialist advice, we will agree with you the adjustments that we will make.

b. We will meet with you to make sure that the adjustments are working for you and us. If any modifications are needed, or if anything new needs to be put in place, we will discuss that with you.

5.6. Step 4

a. We will meet with you on an ongoing basis to check that your symptoms are being managed effectively.

b. You may find that your symptoms change over time. Please tell us if that happens so we can consider further or alternative adjustments. Once your symptoms pass, we expect you to tell us, and we may discuss with you removing the adjustments in place.

5.7. We may need to consult with [*occupational health*] [*your doctor*] at various points to make sure everything is being done that should be done.

5.8. We are aware that you may be indirectly affected by menopause. It may directly affect a loved one or family member, and this may cause concern or distress. We are committed to supporting you too. We urge you to talk to [*a member of HR*] so we can discuss how we might best support you.

6. Our expectations of staff

6.1. We may not be able to tell you about any menopause-related issues that a particular colleague is experiencing. We need you to accept that and respect their privacy.

6.2. Employees must treat each other fairly. Any unfavourable treatment, harassment, teasing or inappropriate comments in relation to menopause or a colleague's symptoms could constitute age, disability or sex discrimination. You are expected to treat each other with respect and compassion. We have a zero-tolerance policy on bullying and harassment (please see our [*Harassment & Bullying Policy*] for more information).

6.3. If you treat a colleague badly (including making unwanted comments or jokes) because of their menopause symptoms, you could be disciplined.

7. Useful links and contacts

7.1. The following internal policies contain additional information and guidance:

a. [*Disciplinary Policy*]

b. [*Flexible Working Policy*]

c. [*Equal Opportunities Policy*]

d. [*Harassment & Bullying Policy*]

e. [*Data Protection Policy*]

f. [*Insert details of any other relevant policies here.*]

7.2. There are lots of web-based resources where you can find support and information. Examples include:

a. https://www.nhs.uk/conditions/menopause

b. https://www.themenopausecharity.org

8. Administration of the Menopause Policy

8.1. [*Insert relevant person or department*] is responsible for the administration of the Menopause Policy. Should you have any feedback, please contact [*insert contact details*].

Appendix 2

Menopause-friendly workplace self-assessment tool

This is a self-assessment tool for businesses to evaluate their current support for menopausal employees and identify areas for improvement.

Rate your business's performance in each area using the following scale:

1 – Not implemented
2 – Partially implemented
3 – Fully implemented

Policy and awareness

1. We have a specific menopause policy in place. [ ]
2. Menopause awareness training is provided to all managers. [ ]
3. We have open discussions about menopause in the workplace. [ ]

Workplace adjustments

4. We offer flexible working arrangements for menopausal employees. [ ]

5. Our office environment can be adjusted for temperature control. [ ]
6. We provide access to quiet areas for rest or privacy. [ ]

Health and wellbeing support

7. We offer access to occupational health services for menopause-related issues. [ ]
8. Mental health support is available for menopausal employees. [ ]
9. We provide information on menopause symptoms and management. [ ]

Communication and culture

10. Our workplace culture is supportive of discussing menopause openly. [ ]
11. We have a clear process for employees to request menopause-related support. [ ]
12. Senior leadership actively promotes menopause awareness. [ ]

Performance management

13. Our performance review process considers potential menopause-related challenges. [ ]
14. Managers are trained to have sensitive conversations about menopause. [ ]

15. We have a system to monitor and address menopause-related absences. [ ]

Scoring and action planning

Total your scores:

- 36-45: Excellent support; continue to maintain and improve.
- 26-35: Good support; identify specific areas for enhancement.
- 15-25: Basic support; develop a comprehensive action plan.
- Below 15: Immediate action required; prioritise policy development and training.

For any items scored 1 or 2, create specific action items to address these areas. Consider forming a working group to implement improvements and regularly reassess your business's support for menopausal employees.

Also by Daniel Barnett

Preventing and DEFENDING Employee STRESS CLAIMS
Changing Terms and Conditions
HR Hazards
Model answers to 70 HR problems
Employment Tribunal COMPENSATION
Menopause and the Workplace
DANIEL BARNETT

LBC

Dear HR Professional,

I take my hat off to you.

Having supported the HR community for so many years, I know It's a challenging job you do, sometimes under really difficult circumstances.

The tricky HR issues you have to handle must take up a tremendous amount of your time, your energy and your brain power. I bet it can be exhausting for you to work under that level of pressure.

Being An HR Professional In Today's Business Environment Is TOUGH!

Maintaining your high standards of professionalism must be a real struggle, especially when your efforts and expertise often go unappreciated.

I'll wager you have to make decisions on challenging HR situations you've sometimes never encountered before. Even if you're part of a team, it must sometimes feel like you're working in isolation.

With so much complexity and ambiguity, do you ever find you're not clear whether you're doing the right thing when there's so much to think about?

I expect it can be draining too. You've got to make tough decisions which may be unpopular.

The pressure's on you to ensure people are treated fairly while the business complies with its legal obligations.

It's a thankless task, especially if you've got grief coming at you from all sides.

Doubt can creep in too. Even though you're an extremely competent professional, you might even begin to question yourself... What if you've got it wrong?

You've got to cope with all that, whilst constantly having to convince any doubting stakeholders you're adding value to the business.

That pressure must take its toll on you.

You wouldn't be human if it didn't cause you tension, stress or even worse!

Being the caring professional you are, I bet you often take work home with you.

If You're Not Careful The Stress WILL Creep Up On You

And I don't just mean opening your laptop on your couch when everyone else is watching Eastenders.

We all know of families and relationships that come a poor second to the pressures and challenges faced at work.

Yours too..?

But does it have to be that way?

Should you feel the responsibility of the HR world is entirely on your shoulders and that you've got to bear that burden alone?

The answer is a firm no.

It doesn't have to be like that.

There Is An Answer To Help Make Your Work & Your Life Much Easier For You

There's a place you can get all the help, support, advice and encouragement you need to ease the constant pressure you have to bear.

It's called the HR Inner Circle.

It will lift the burden you're carrying by giving you swift access to comprehensive resources and live practical guidance you can implement right away.

It's information I know will save you time, energy and effort.

It's a vibrant, active community of caring, like minded HR professionals willing to help you.

There are resources packed full of practical, actionable advice for you that's difficult to find anywhere else.

And it doesn't matter what you're working on.

Whether it be workforce engagement, attracting and keeping talent, diversity and inclusion or employee health and well being, you'll find support for all of that.

You're covered even if you're working on one of those tricky, sensitive, people problems you never see coming until they land squarely on your plate.

Timely Support To Make Your Job Easier, Can Be Rapidly Found In The HR Inner Circle

As a member of the HR Inner Circle, to get the support you want…

…just ask.

Your first port of call is the vibrant Facebook group, bursting at the seams with incredible HR professionals like you.

Just post your question and let it bubble and simmer in the collective genius of the group.

By the end of the day, you'll have at least 3-5 comments on your post, often more.

You'll get relevant, insightful and practical guidance that comes from the hard earned experience of your fellow members.

Often you'll get a response within a couple of hours. Sometimes you'll get an answer within minutes - even if it's late in the evening!

This highly active community never fails to astound me with just how willing they are to help fellow HR professionals like you.

They readily and generously share their hard earned knowledge and experience.

You Can Get Answers From <u>Real People</u> Quickly AND From Our Extensive Resource Library Too

> …really important for someone working on their own who needs to check things out, or just bounce a few ideas around.
>
> - Quentin Colborn
> Director, QC People Management Ltd

While you wait for a response from the Facebook group, you'll likely find answers in the resource-rich members' vault on our secure online portal as well.

It takes just 2 clicks and a quick keyword search using our Rapid Results Search Tool.

You'll instantly find precisely where your topic is covered in our extensive back catalogue of monthly magazines and audio seminars.

In under 30 seconds you can find exactly what you're after.

It's that quick and easy.

...And if you need a specific legal insight?

Then pose your question live to an expert employment lawyer in our monthly Q&A session.

It'll either be me or one of my prominent contemporaries. You'll get your answer immediately without having to pay any legal costs.

If you can't wait, you'll find where it's been answered before with a quick search of previous Q&A sessions.

Our clever index system means you can find a question, and in a single click get straight to the recorded answer.

But perhaps you need to dive deep and explore the different options open to you to solve a particularly tricky problem?

Then join one of our monthly HR Huddles. There you can run your specific situation past other HR professionals.

They'll offer their insights, share their experience and work WITH you to find a solution that works FOR you.

You'll find all of this in one convenient place - the HR Inner Circle.

It's Been A Labour Of Love Putting The HR Inner Circle Together So It Works For Professionals Like You

> **It's great to see that we all experience tricky cases from time to time.**
>
> - Annabelle Carey
> Managing Consultant, HR Services Partnership

I've spent years practising law and have become recognised as one of the UK's leading employment law barristers. I've even got my own radio show!

But more importantly for you, I've also developed another skill.

It's bringing useful employment expertise AND practical experience together in a way that supports busy, overworked (and sometimes stressed) HR professionals like you.

Everything you're likely to need is **literally at your fingertips**.

This will save you **time**, **energy** and **effort**.

Being a member also means your business and clients will see you as even MORE INFORMED about the intricacies of employment law.

They'll marvel at how well you keep up to date when you're busy working so hard for them.

You'll be seen making quicker decisions and implementing effective solutions to accelerate the growth of the organisation.

You'll make impressive time and cost savings for the business.

And those tricky, off-piste situations you've never come across before..?

Well, nothing will faze you, because you're backed up by an HR support system second to none.

But more importantly, you'll feel that pressure gently ease off.

With the relief you'll feel knowing that such great help and guidance is just a few minutes, you'll wonder how you survived without it!

That's Why I'm Inviting You To Join And Reap The Many Rewards Of Membership

WWW.HRINNERCIRCLE.CO.UK

Here's what you get when you join the HR Inner Circle:

Benefit #1- you'll get unlimited access to the hugely popular HR Inner Circle Facebook Private Group

- Tap into the vast wealth of knowledge, experience, insight and wisdom of the top 0.5% of your profession at any time, day or night.
- In less than 5 minutes you can post ANY HR question and get insightful answers and suggestions in a couple of hours or less, from some of the best in your profession.
- Fast track your impact by discovering effective shortcuts and workarounds from HR people who've been "there" and done "it".
- Expand and deepen your network of like minded individuals, secure in the knowledge they're as dedicated and as ambitious as you.

- Increase your prestige with your colleagues and stakeholders by being part of such an exclusive and prominent HR community.
- Gain confidence in your judgment and decisions by using the highly responsive community as a sounding board for your ideas.

Benefit #2 - you'll receive 11 copies of the HR Inner Circular Magazine every year

- Enjoy that satisfying "THUD" on your door mat every month when the postman delivers your very own copy of the HR Inner Circular magazine.
- Quickly discover exactly what the law says about key issues affecting HR professionals around the UK like you.
- Get concise and practical guidance on how employment law applies to the challenging situations and circumstances you deal with every day.
- Avoid the mistakes of others by applying the lessons from the in depth analysis of real life case studies.
- Benefit from a legal deep dive by the UK's leading employment law barrister into a topical employment question posed by a fellow member (perhaps you!).
- Review a summary of recent important Facebook Group discussions worthy of sharing, that you may have missed.
- Explore a range of related and relevant topics useful for your practice and your broader professional development.

> **The magazine is really informative, the Facebook group such a community, and I think exceptional value for money.**
>
> \- Lis Moore
> Head of Advisory & Support Services,
> Society of Local Council Clerks

Benefit #3 - Monthly Audio Seminars

- A 60 minute legal deep dive by me into an important subject relevant to you and your practice.
- Professionally recorded content recorded exclusively for the HR Inner Circle - you'll not find this information anywhere else.
- Carefully structured content that's easy to consume, understand and apply in your work as an HR professional.
- Episodes delivered every month so you can stay current on the latest issues affecting HR professionals.
- The convenience of listening to the recording online or downloading the mp3 for later enjoyment at a time suitable to your busy schedule (perfect for any commute).

Benefit #4 - you get an exclusive invite to a live online Q&A Session every fortnight, led by an expert employment lawyer

- Gain 60 minutes of live and direct access to the sharpest legal minds from my secret little black book of contacts.
- Get answers to your knottiest employment law questions, and solutions to your trickiest HR problems, from some of the brightest employment lawyers in the UK.
- Avoid having to pay the £300-£400 it would cost you to ask a lawyer your question outside of the HR Inner Circle.
- Benefit from valuable insights from the answers given to other members.
- If you can't attend live, watch the recording when it's convenient for you.
- Quickly access the recorded answer to any question asked in the session by simply clicking the question index for that session.

- Save time by downloading the session transcription to scan-read at a time suitable for you.

Benefit #5 - join a live Monthly Huddle with other HR Professionals to solve your most challenging HR problems

- Attend your very own mini-mastermind group of highly qualified, highly regarded and experienced fellow HR professionals to "group think" through an issue you're facing right now.
- Develop bespoke solutions to the unique problems and challenges you have to deal with in a safe, supportive and confidential environment.
- Feel safe knowing these online zoom calls are NOT recorded to respect the sensitivity of issues addressed and the privacy of those involved. [NOTE - a professional transcriber attends and takes written notes. An anonymised summary is then made available to the membership]
- Recent Huddle topics included changing employee benefits, mandatory vaccination, career breaks, sickness during disciplinaries, effective worker forums and hybrid working arrangements.

Benefit #6 - access our Templates & Resources Centre

- Gain immediate access to our library of the most popular and frequently used forms, assessments, agreements, checklists, letter templates, questionnaires and reports to help the busiest HR professionals save time and get things done quicker and easier.
- Download them as Word documents, so you can edit and personalise them to fit your business needs
- New templates added every single month

Benefit #7 - build your own Employment Law Library

- We send you several brand-new books on employment law several times each year
- Acquire your own physical library of concise, easy-to-read and fully updated textbooks
- Recent titles include Hiring Staff, Managing Sickness Absence, Spotting Malingering and Resolving Grievances

Benefit #8 - free Ticket to our Annual Conference

- The perfect opportunity to extend your personal network of fellow HR professionals.
- Meet up face to face with the people who've been supporting you in the Facebook Group and HR Huddles so you can deepen those connections even further.
- Gather key insights and takeaways to help you personally and professionally from some of the best speakers on the circuit. Previous speakers have covered motivation, dealing with difficult people, goal setting and productivity, decision making and social media marketing.
- Get instant access to recordings of all previous conferences so even if you can't attend in person, you can benefit from the event in your own time.
- Includes probably the best conference lunch you'll ever have - a bold claim I know, but we use outstanding caterers.

> **It never ceases to amaze me the amount of time and effort people put into the Facebook group, sharing their experiences, advice, and sage words of wisdom.**
>
> **- Emma Lister**
> HR Consultant, SME HR Services

Benefit #9 - your Personal Concierge will help you get the best out of your membership

- You get personal access to Nina who'll point you in the direction of exactly where to find what you need. She's supported hundreds of members over the 5 years she's been part of the team.
- Nina also works closely with the 11 back office staff that support the operation. In the extremely unlikely event she doesn't know where something is, she knows who will.

HOW MUCH DOES JOINING THE HR INNER CIRCLE COST?

There's no doubt in my mind the annual value of membership benefits is in the many thousands of pounds range.

But you're not going to pay anywhere near that.

Let me remind you of what that small monthly fee gives you every year

Access to the private Facebook Group	INCLUDED
HR Inner Circular Magazine subscription	INCLUDED
Monthly Audio Seminars	INCLUDED
Live Q&A sessions	INCLUDED
Monthly HR Huddles	INCLUDED
Templates & Resources Centre	INCLUDED
Employment Law Library	INCLUDED
Free ticket to the HR Inner Circle Annual Conference	INCLUDED
Your Personal Membership Concierge	INCLUDED

TOTAL PRICELESS

Another way of looking at your investment is this:

Because access to what you need is so quick…

Join today and that price is fixed for as long as you remain a member. You'll always pay the same, even if we increase the price to new members (which we regularly do).

…it's like having your very own part time, legally trained, assistant HR Business Partner, just waiting to provide you with all the answers you need…

WWW.HRINNERCIRCLE.CO.UK

Plus, With Membership Of The HR Inner Circle, You'll Also Get These 4 Additional Resources For FREE!

Additional Resource #1 - Handling Awkward Conversations

A video case study masterclass you can share with managers to train them to handle awkward staff disciplinary, performance and attitude problems. A huge time saver for you.

Additional Resource #2 - 6 x HR Employment Online Courses

Immediate, on demand access to six thorough, online HR courses (with more constantly added), including Employment Tribunal Compensation, Chat GPT for HR Professionals, Deconstructing TUPE, Changing Terms & Conditions, Unconscious Bias At Work and Handling Grievances.

Additional Resource #3 - Free listing on the Register of Investigators

Advertise your professional investigations service in our member's portal.

Additional Resource #4 - Significant discounts on sets of policies, contracts, and other courses.

Get member discounts on my Getting Redundancy Right and HR Policies products as well as other price reductions as new products are released.

WWW.HRINNERCIRCLE.CO.UK

> It's a really good investment. The support you get from other Facebook group members is fantastic. Whatever your question, someone will know the answer. Access to Daniel's experience and knowledge through the podcasts and Q&A is invaluable too.
>
> - Tracy Madgwick
> HR Consultant, Crafnant HR

I'm So Confident Joining The HR Inner Circle Is The Right Decision For You, Here's My

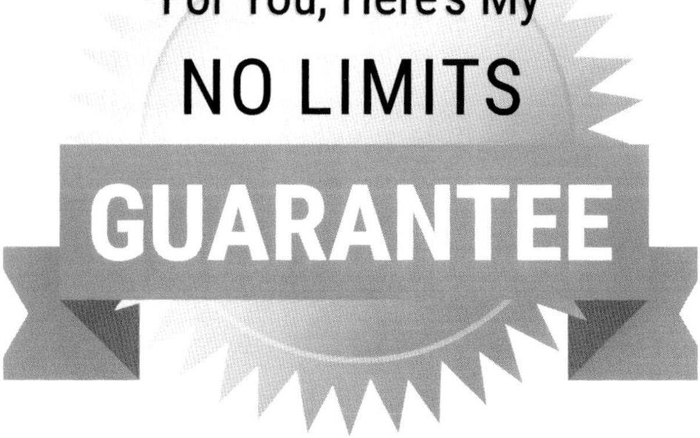

Take action and join the HR Inner Circle **now**.

If you're not 100% satisfied with your investment, you can cancel at ANY time.

Just tell us, and your membership will end immediately. No long-term contracts. No notice periods. No fuss.

I'm comfortable doing this because I know once you join, you'll find the support, the information and the strategies so useful, you'll never want to leave.

Before you decide though, let me be very clear about membership of the HR Inner Circle.

It's only for ambitious and dedicated HR professionals who want to accelerate and increase their impact by plugging into an HR ecosystem with its finger firmly on the pulse of what's working right now in HR.

If you're just plodding along and are content with just getting by, then this is probably not for you.